Dear God,

.... If I Have To Go To Bed ...... Will You Come Too?

Annie

I wish that I were all grown-up.
I'd like to stay up late.
Dear God, I have too much to do
to be in bed by eight.

I love to see the moon at night
and watch it for awhile.
And like a friend it often has
a big and gentle smile.

Dear God,
... I'M SO GLAD
THAT YOU DON'T TURN
OUT
THE MOON

Annie

Sometimes I can be frightened by the noises in the night. I'm glad that you are by my side until the morning light.

Dear God,

..... I'm not afraid of the dark ...... but would you talk to me?

Annie

Good night, Dear God.

It's time to sleep.

Please keep me in your care.

Bless mom and dad

and all my friends.

And bless my teddy bear.

Dear God, when I'm asleep at night,
I still know how to play.
I dream of castles,
kings, and queens,
and places far away.

Dear God,
...OK,
WHAT WILL WE
DREAM ABOUT
TONIGHT?

Annie

My mouth tells me
it's time to sleep.
It makes a great big O.
When yawning starts
I close my eyes,
and off to sleep I go.

Dear GOD,

.....DO YOU SEND YAWNS JUST TO MAKE ME SLEEPY?

Annie

Now I lay me down to sleep
to rest my tired eyes.
Dear God, I'll see you once again
tomorrow when I rise.

Dear GOD,

... It's time to say good-night ..... see you in the morning

Annie